The Unofficial Field Manual to Geocaching

Also by Robyn C. Broyles

My Puzzle Fix, Volume 1

THE
UNOFFICIAL
FIELD MANUAL TO
⊕EOCACHING

ROBYN C. BROYLES

Sparkitect Media
Houston, Texas

796.5
B

ISBN-13: 978-0615632919
ISBN-10: 0615632912

A.M.D.G.

To Max, Roman, and Zander,
my favorite geocaching buddies.

Contents

How to Use This Manual

This book is designed to be carried by geocachers into the field. Small and lightweight, it's made to fit into your pocket, and it contains information useful to the geocacher on the trail, from etiquette rules to distance conversions. It also contains information about geocaching websites, how to plan your trip, and how to hide your own geocache, including a note you can copy and place in your cache to explain what it is.

If you come across an unfamiliar term while reading, turn to page 77 and look it up in the glossary. For information on a particular topic, turn past the glossary to the index. And if you need to record something, jot it down in the Field Notes.

1 · What Is Geocaching?

Geocaching is the hobby of hiding and seeking geocaches, containers with known latitude and longitude that hold logbooks and sometimes other items, using a handheld receiver for the Global Positioning System (GPS). Geocaching is an activity full of contrasts. It is both a social sport, in that many players hide caches to share with the community, and a solitary activity, in that most players work alone or in very small groups. It is both a high-tech hobby, requiring the use of the ad-vanced technology of global positioning, and a primal pastime, well-suited to those who enjoy wide open spaces and the great outdoors. It's a game that can be played with virtually nothing but a GPS receiver, or it can involve expensive gear and foreign travel. It can be cutthroat or non-competitive, according to each player's preference.

A geocache in its basic form is a weatherproof container, stashed somewhere outdoors but not buried in the earth, with a logbook that visitors sign. Some caches also contain small trinkets, usually of low cost, for trade. To make finding caches more challenging for players, and to protect the caches from the uninitiated (often called "muggles"), the containers are hidden and/or camouflaged

Benefits of Geocaching

Geocaching brings health benefits along with it. As a leisure activity, it can lower stress, and traveling to caches on foot makes good exercise. The rush of finding a geocache is a psychological reward, and when caching is done in pairs or small groups, it becomes a form of socialization.

Geocaching connects players with the local area. By selective placement of caches, players can call attention to little-known aspects of local lore. Historical people and events are connected with certain locations, and these are popular sites for geocaches that provide an account of that connection. Some caches highlight under-appreciated areas with beautiful scenery or incredible plants, rocks, or wildlife.

1.1 GPS Technology

The system of global positioning satellites was originally developed by the U.S. military to provide precise position data. In practice, the Global Positioning System (GPS) provides accuracy of up to about three to four feet.

Though the first GPS satellite was launched in 1978, geocaching did not become possible until May 2, 2000, when accurate satellite data was made publicly available. The first geocache was placed the very next day in Beavercreek, Oregon. Today there are millions of geocaches located all over the world and on all seven continents, and there is even a geocache on the International Space Station.

GPS satellites continuously transmit signals that include both their position and the time with a high degree of precision. GPS receivers use this information to calculate the distance to the satellites. With signals from a minimum of four satellites (three for position data and one for error correction), the receiver can calculate its own location on the earth's surface in three dimensions: latitude, lon-

Block IIR(M) type GPS satellite

gitude, and elevation. Only the first two values are of interest to geocachers.

Wide Area Augmentation System

The Wide Area Augmentation System (WAAS) is a supplement to the GPS designed to improve its accuracy. It uses a combination of ground-based stations and its own satellites to detect small differences in GPS signals and to issue corrections. Many newer GPS receivers can use WAAS data to improve position accuracy.

Other Global Navigation Systems

The United States is not the only government to create a system like the GPS. Russia has established the Global Navigation Satellite System (GLONASS), whose data became public in 2007. Some GPS receivers are able to use GLONASS data in addition to GPS data. Europe, India, and China have similar systems in various stages of planning and construction.

How Coordinates Work

Latitude (φ, phi) and longitude (λ, lambda) are measured in degrees, units equal to 1/360 of a circle. Latitude lines are imaginary circles parallel to the equator and are measured starting from the equator all the way to each pole (0° to 90°). Longitude meridians are imaginary great circles passing through the poles and are measured, by convention, starting from the prime meridian passing through Greenwich, England (0° to 180°).

Coordinates are given either in decimal degrees (the number of degrees to four or five decimal places) or, more commonly in geocaching, in degrees and minutes (one minute is equal to 1/60 degree). In geocaching, the third format for coordinates—degrees, minutes, and seconds (where one second is equal to 1/60 minute)—is never used. Regardless of format, a coordinate always includes a direction (either north or south, or east or west). A position consists of two coordinates, one for latitude and one for longitude.

1.2 Geocaching Etiquette

Geocaching is fun because of the contributions of many different players. Certain etiquette rules have developed to keep the game worthwhile. Like most etiquette rules, they can be summed up by the golden rule: treat others as you would yourself be treated.

Geocachers' Creed

The Geocachers' Creed is a voluntary code of ethics developed by the geocaching community and recommended for all geocachers. The text of the seven-point creed is as follows:

When placing or seeking geocaches, I will:
- Not endanger myself or others
- Observe all laws & rules of the area
- Respect property rights and seek permission where appropriate
- Avoid causing disruptions or public alarm

- Minimize my and others' impact on the environment
- Be considerate of others
- Protect the integrity of the game pieces

Items in Caches

Items for trade are common in regular and large cache containers. These items add a little extra fun to the game for some players, but it is never required to deal with trade items. Typically they have little intrinsic value and often consist of small toys and party favors. No trade item should ever be removed from a cache unless something of equal or greater value is left behind. Though some geocachers leave money in exchange for trade items they take, this practice is frowned upon.

Geocaching should not be used to promote an agenda or business. Don't leave items (like coupons) in caches specifically to promote your organization, although business cards are occasionally seen in caches, as are religious items.

Trackables (traveling items that are tracked online) are not considered trade items and do not fall under the rules of trade etiquette. They should not be collected or kept, as each one belongs to the person who first purchased and placed it. If a

---

cache has several trackables, don't take them all unless you are also leaving trackables behind. Leave at least one or two behind for other cachers to enjoy. For more information on trackables, see page 32.

Logs

There are two logs for each geocache. The first, also called the logbook, is a notebook (or, in smaller caches, a single piece of paper) in which cache visitors record their name and the date of the find. If space permits, you may make comments about your experience, but for small logbooks, record only your name and the date. You can use your real name, your online handle, or both.

The second log is found online. (On Geocaching.com, each entry into this list is called a log, and the collection is called the log entries.) When you are at home after geocaching (or while you are still in the field if you are using a device with mobile Internet access), you should record your visit in the online log. It's preferred that you always add a comment or story about your experience. For uneventful finds, at least thank the owner for the cache (the acronyms TFTC, "thanks for the cache," and TFTH, "thanks for the hide," are common.)

If you cannot find a cache, it's courteous to leave an online log entry anyway to let the owner know you could not find it. You may have just overlooked it, but if several cachers in a row post DNF (did not find) log entries, the owner will usually investigate the cache to make sure it has not disappeared or been moved.

If a cache is damaged, has a full log, or otherwise needs attention from the owner, you can post an online log entry indicating that the cache needs maintenance. Doing so will take the cache off many geocachers' lists, so only do this if the owner's attention is really needed.

Modifying Caches

Never move a geocache. If you think it is in the wrong location, make a note in the online log, perhaps including better coordinates. If you can repair a mildly damaged cache (for example, replacing a torn plastic bag), you may do so. Many geocachers believe that major repairs, however, should be attempted only by the cache owners because only they receive notifications about problems with their caches. A cache that is not being maintained should be archived (retired), not restored by others.

CITO bag found in a geocache

Cache In Trash Out

Cache In Trash Out, or CITO, is the habit of cleaning up the area around caches you visit. Many geocachers carry plastic bags with them to every cache for CITO. Occasionally large-scale CITO events are organized for the geocaching community, providing a chance to meet each other and to clean up a large area such as a park.

2 · Getting Ready

The first step to geocaching is to get a GPS receiver (GPSr) and open an account on a geocaching website. Other equipment besides a GPS receiver can make your trip much more fruitful. Before you look for any geocaches, though, you have to decide how thoroughly to plan your trip. And it always starts with a visit to the Internet.

2.1 Geocaching Websites

Geocache information is shared via the Internet. There are several different geocaching websites, each with different site ownership and philosophies. These websites include NaviCache (www.navicache.com) and Open Caching (www.opencaching.com), but by far the most active and best developed site is Groundspeak's Geocaching. com. This guide is focused on playing the game through this site, although the information here can be applied to geocaching through other sites as well.

Geocaching.com

At Geocaching.com, you can play for free by signing up for a Basic Membership, although many site features (including access to certain caches) require the purchase of a Premium Membership, currently (U.S.) $10.00 per quarter or $30.00 per year. With a Basic Membership, you can search for caches near a location (but cannot narrow down search results using keywords or parameters) and access coordinate, description, and log data for universal-access caches. Premium Members have the option to make any cache they hide a Premium Member Cache, not accessible to Basic Members. These caches appear in everyone's search results, but when Basic Members click on one, they are re-directed to a page encouraging them to buy a Premium Membership to gain access to the co-ordinates, description, and logs.

Other features of Geocaching.com include the ability to download cache data in files to be up-

loaded to your GPS receiver. These files can be collected individually, one file per cache. They have
two file formats: .loc, which includes only basic
cache data like coordinates, and .gpx, which also
includes cache descriptions and logs. For Premium
Mem-bers only, data from many caches can be
saved in a single file called a Pocket Query. Pocket
Queries can contain up to 1000 caches.

The Cache Page

On Geocaching.com, each geocache has its
own web page with a wealth of information at the
top, including the cache name, its coordinates, its
serial number (called the GC code because it always starts with the letters GC), its owner, and the
date it was hidden. Also available are information
on search difficulty, terrain difficulty, and container
size.

Under this information is the description, written
by the owner; a hint, if the owner has given one;
and log entries. To prevent spoilers, the hint is in a
code called a ROT13 cipher, in which each letter
stands for the letter 13 places before or after it in
the alphabet. It can be decoded online with a
click of the mouse button, or deciphered in the field

without much effort. The key for decoding ROT13 is found on page 71.

Two thumbnail maps are available on the right side of the page. The smaller one is at the top; the larger one, a little way down, includes a link to view the location of that cache and all other nearby caches on a full-screen interactive map.

The cache page also includes information on trackables currently in the cache, although this information is not always accurate.

When you are ready to log a cache, visit its page and click the "log your visit" link at the right side of the page. You will land on a page with a web form for you to record your log. You will have to select the type of log entry from a drop-down menu. Make sure the date is correct for the date you visited the cache, even if you are posting your log at a later date. Note whether you dropped off any trackables or merely brought them along with you ("visited"), if you have any. You have the option of adding an updated set of coordinates to your log entry.

Each cache page has the shortcut URL http://coord.info/GC1234, where GC1234 is re-placed by the cache's particular GC code.

Mobile Internet Access

If your GPS receiver does not display all the cache information found in a .gpx file, you can use a smartphone with Internet access to look up descriptions and logs in the field. This capability can be invaluable, especially for impulsive geocaching trips. Not all mobile Internet devices have a browser that can manage the main website at www.geocaching.com. An alternative mobile website is available at wap.geocaching.com. From the mobile site, after logging in, you can look up individual caches to read the description and logs, mark caches as found, and search for a list of nearby caches. If you have a username and password that are long and difficult to enter on your mobile device, consider creating a second account with an easy-to-enter username and password. If you have a Premium Membership, however, remember that this method will only give you mobile access to Basic Membership information unless you buy a second Premium Membership.

2.2 Planning Your Trip

There are two general planning strategies for geocaching. Your personal plan or style will probably fall on a spectrum between these two extremes: precisely planned and impulsive. Remember that these two strategies are just approaches, not firm procedures. You can take an approach that falls anywhere in the middle of that spectrum, incorporating some planning into your trip while leaving parts of it up to chance.

Planning Precisely

If you are a planner and don't like to meet unexpected obstacles, use this checklist to make sure you have anticipated every aspect of your trip:

- Allow enough time before a trip to plan.
- Read the descriptions and logs to make sure there are no unexpected conditions and that the cache has been found recently by other cachers (a cache that nobody has found recently is more likely to be missing when you arrive).
- Check the weather forecast and make sure conditions will be good for the duration of your trip.
- Mark your route on a map, noting each cache along the way. Check to see if road construction or other delays might affect your route.
- Plan for any breaks or stops you might take and estimate the amount of time each leg of the trip

will take. Make a note of how far each cache is from a good parking area, and allow enough time to hike there and back, as well as to search at ground zero. Add extra time for unforeseen delays.

- Make a list of what to bring with you, and pack carefully using the list.
- If you have a Premium Membership at Geocaching.com, create a Pocket Query and review it to make sure it includes all the caches you want to find, then upload it to your GPS receiver. If your device has the ability to use data besides the basic cache coordinates, difficulty, and container size information, make sure you use the .gpx format in order to capture cache descriptions and logs. Using this method, you can take advantage of so-called paperless geocaching without the need for mobile Internet access. If your device cannot use this extra information, print out each cache page including at least five or ten log entries for each cache on your list.

Impulsive Geocaching

Much of the fun of the hobby, according to some geocachers, lies in encountering the unex-

---

pected. If you prefer to "go with the flow," then try "impulsive geocaching." Go to an area where you are unfamiliar with the local caches and turn on your GPS receiver (preloaded with a non-specific Pocket Query if necessary), then head for the nearest cache. Be aware of these potential pitfalls of unplanned geocaching trips:

• You will find a smaller percentage of the caches you look for than you would find if you planned carefully. By not researching caches ahead of time, you will sometimes find yourself searching diligently for caches that are not there or that require special knowledge to find.

• If you have one, carry a smartphone or other mobile device that can access the Internet in the field. If you are stymied at the site of a cache you have not researched, you may want to check the description and logs for hints before you give up and move on.

• Bring a map of the local area if at all possible. If you really want an unpredictable experience, you do not have to look at it, but it can be useful if you find yourself in a maze of unfamiliar roadways.

Goals

The only goal you need to have to enjoy geo-caching is to have fun and remember that it's only a game. But many cachers spice up the game by adding additional goals.

- First to find (FTF): Being the first person to find a geocache that has just been published for the first time is a prize sought by many geocachers. To have a reasonable chance at success, you will need to get updates on new caches on a mobile device and be prepared to engage in some impulsive geocaching with no advance warning. A Premium Membership is very helpful, as it allows you to receive instant notification of newly published caches.

- Travel: Some geocachers try to see how many states or countries they can add to their list of places where they have found geocaches.

- Non-traditional caches: These special caches present unique challenges, and focusing just on them is a fun goal. Completing a large multi-cache can be a goal in and of itself, and so can accumulating as many completed puzzle caches and multi-caches as possible.

Transportation

You need a reliable vehicle to get to most caches, even if it just brings you to a trailhead. Bring money for parking, if that is a concern (and always park legally). For many caches, a bicycle may be the only transportation you need.

2.3 Choosing a GPS Receiver

The single item absolutely required for geo-caching is a hand-held device that can determine your latitude and longitude on the earth's surface. Generally this device will be a Global Positioning System receiver (sometimes abbreviated GPSr). Dedicated GPS receivers, some made for general use and others made just for geocaching, are a great choice. Many smartphones have the capability of using GPS data to show your location.

Some smartphones that do not have GPS capability can still be used for geocaching (though not reliably) because they can estimate your position from cell tower data. For example, Groundspeak's geocaching app for Android phones has this capability. If your phone does not have GPS capability, however, you will have the most success at geocaching if you also have a GPS receiver.

How to Buy a GPSr

If you don't already have a GPSr or smartphone with GPS capability, you will need to buy one. You can get a GPSr from outdoors stores or from the Internet. Online, they can be purchased new from any of several Internet retailers; new or used from online auction sites; or used through a private purchase. Beware of purchasing through a website with a sketchy history or from a private individual. For best results, use an established retailer or auction site.

Features

Reviews of various GPS receiver models are not within the scope of this manual. Instead, features commonly available on different devices are explored below.

- Plug and play: GPS receivers made specifically for geocaching may be ready to download cache information right out of the box. Others, including mobile phones, require you to download an app (which may not be free) and install it first.

- Positioning Technology: Besides GPS data, many newer GPSrs can access other data as well. The ability to access information from

WAAS (which improves GPS accuracy) and GLONASS (the Russian counterpart of the Global Positioning System) can give even better results. For example, if your unit can access GLONASS along with GPS, it has more satellites to work from, meaning that it is more likely to find a signal when buildings or heavy tree canopy are blocking part of the sky.

- Ability to enter coordinates: Most GPS receivers allow you to enter coordinates manually, an important feature for finding certain geo-caches. Some of the simplest ones made just for geocaching may only hold cache information downloaded directly from the Internet, meaning that puzzle caches, multi-caches, and newly published caches can be much more chal-lenging to find.

- Computer interface: Units not made with geo-caching in mind may not have a method of interfacing directly with a computer (either a data cable or a wireless communication fea-ture). All geocaches must be entered by hand on these units, and as a result, they are not recommended.

- Map: Most, but not all, GPS receivers have a basemap feature. The map is a valuable resource, although not crucial to successful geo-caching. Those without a map use an ar-row to indicate the direction of the cache.

- Screen: A full-color screen may be marketed as a plus, but in sunlight a monochrome LCD screen may be easier to read. A backlight feature can help with the readability of the screen, both in bright light and in the dark. If your device has a map, screen size is an important consideration.

- Storage: Every GPSr has an upper limit to the amount of cache data it can store, although some units can store additional information on a data card. For carefully planned geocaching trips, this limit may not be important, since every geocache loaded into the unit is chosen ahead of time. For impulsive geocaching, the more storage, the better, since you will not know ahead of time which caches you want to search for.

- Ruggedness: Geocaching is an outdoor activity that often takes place in rough conditions. A good GPSr will be durable enough to survive being dropped on rocky ground or a concrete sidewalk. Consider water-resistance, too. Without this feature, even rainstorms are a danger to your device, let alone being dropped in water.

- Data handling: The best devices for geocaching can handle .loc and .gpx files directly, without the need to install additional software. The ability to make full use of .gpx files is necessary for paperless geocaching.

- Bells and whistles: Higher-end GPS receivers may include many other optional features, each of which adds to the price. Make decisions about advanced features like touch screens, QWERTY keyboards, and cameras based on your needs and budget.

Dedicated GPSr vs. Smartphone

More and more smartphones (such as the iPhone and many Android phones) have built-in GPS receivers and can be used for geocaching. There are a few considerations that will help with the decision of whether to choose a smartphone or a dedicated GPSr—or of whether or not to purchase a dedicated GPSr if you already have a GPS-enabled smartphone.

- Purpose: If you have a limited budget and can only buy one or the other, don't choose a smartphone if you really only want it for geocaching. Dedicated GPS receivers are made for their purpose and typically have better GPS hardware. On the other hand, if you will really find the features of a smartphone use-ful, this choice is a good compromise.

- Navigation methods: Units made specifically for GPS may also be able to use WAAS and the Russian GLONASS navigation system for even better locational accuracy, although some of the newest smartphones are now manufactured with GLONASS capability as well.

- Battery: A smartphone usually must be re-charged via a charging cable, and geo-caching can drain the battery heavily. Many GPS receivers, on the other hand, use AA or AAA batteries, which can be changed quickly in the field.

- Planning approach: Dedicated GPS receivers generally must be plugged into a computer in order to acquire geocache data. Since smart-phones are Internet-capable computers them-selves, this step can be eliminated, which is great for impulsive geocaching and for the goal of being the first to find new caches.

2.4 Using Your GPSr

Get familiar with your GPS receiver, its user inter-face, and its features. Normally, you need to load geocache data to your GPS receiver before you go geocaching. (Instructions on how to find a geo-cache if you cannot enter cache data for some reason are found on pages 66–67.)

Loading Cache Data onto a GPSr

Most GPS receivers allow the user to input co-ordinates manually. This is necessary in the case of puzzle caches and multi-caches because the cache pages do not include complete and ac-curate coordinate information for these cache types.

From Geocaching.com, you also have the op-tion to send the data for each cache directly to DeLorme, Magellan, and Garmin GPS receivers (you will have to download a plugin the first time you do this). First attach your device to your com-puter using the appropriate cable. On the search results page, at the far right of each listing is an icon of an arrow pointing to a mobile device. Click these icons to load caches to your GPSr one at a time. You can also upload a cache from the cache page. Click the link called "Send to GPS."

This method is slow because it loads caches only one at a time.

For other GPS receivers, you will have to save the cache data on your computer's hard drive first, then upload the file to your GPSr. Basic Members at Geocaching.com have access only to a .loc file, which includes the basic information on caches, such as coordinates, but no detailed information. Premium Members have access to a .gpx file, which includes the description and recent log entries.

Premium Members also have the capability of saving many caches (up to 1000) in one .gpx file using a Pocket Query. You can set the parameters for the Pocket Query search, such as including only caches you haven't found, only caches of a certain size, and/or only caches with certain attributes. By far, this is the fastest way to save caches on your GPSr. It also facilitates impulsive geocaching because you don't have to find each cache online before you go out to search for it.

Live–Enabled Geocaching

Several geocaching applications make it possible to load data on the nearest caches in real-time. These applications are available for smartphones and make use of several types of location data to determine your position.   Live–enabled geocaching applications are great for impulsive geocaching.

2.5 Items for Caches

Most geocaches (other than micros) contain items in addition to the logbook. These items are meant to be shared with the geocaching community.

Trade Items

Most geocachers carry a few items for trade (swag), although this is not a necessary part of geocaching.   Most of the trade items you encounter will not have much monetary value (usually under $1.00). You should always leave an item of equal or greater value behind for every item to you take.

Buy trade items at discount department stores, party stores, dollar stores, or anywhere else you find inexpensive toys or collectibles. Here are just a few examples of possible trade items:

- Army men
- Balls
- Bean bags
- Die-cast cars

Example trade items

- Dolls and action figures
- Erasers
- Jewelry (costume or toy jewelry)
- Mardi Gras coins (doubloons)
- Pencil sharpeners
- Pens or pencils
- Plastic animals
- Toys that come with fast-food kids' meals
- Whistles and other noisemakers

Some geocachers use trade items as personal "calling cards." You can buy or make any kind of signature item you like. Examples are beaded key chains, painted rocks, pre-printed pencils, and wooden nickels. Pathtags (www.pathtags.com)

are enamel-painted, serially numbered coins that serve as unique "calling cards" for cachers. They should not be confused with trackables like geocoins. Pathtags can be collected and kept following the etiquette for all trade items, and can even be registered online using the serial numbers.

Certain trade items should be avoided. Never place any kind of food in a geocache; it's likely to spoil and attract animals. Balloons are made of biodegradable latex and don't last long inside caches, and paper products (such as trading cards) tend to be very susceptible to water damage. Never place anything dangerous, illegal, or fragile in a geocache. Remember that kids visit geocaches too, so keep all items family-friendly.

Trackables

Trackables add another dimension to the game of geocaching. A trackable is an item with a serial number that can be logged and tracked on a geocaching website. The two types of trackables are geocoins (usually metallic, and sometimes custom minted) and Travel Bugs (usually aluminum key chains attached to another object). A trackable has two numbers: the public code used online by anyone who wants to follow the item's progress, and a private tracking code printed directly on the item. Each trackable's web page has the shortcut URL http://coord.info/TB1234, where TB1234 is replaced by the trackable's own public code.

If you find a trackable, you can take it from the cache without following the usual etiquette for trade items. Remember that it is not yours to keep; you should only take a trackable if you expect to be able to place it in another geocache within about two weeks.

Once you have a trackable, log it online using the tracking code printed on the item. (From Geocaching.com, find the menu item called "Find Trackables.") Don't use the public number found online. Leave a log entry just as you would for a geocache. Also check the trackable's web page to find out if the owner has any goals for the item. For example, an owner may want their trackable to travel to a specific location or to visit as many puzzle caches as possible. If possible, try to help the owner achieve the goal when you replace the trackable in a geocache.

You can buy your own trackables and set goals for them. Remember that you won't be able to keep them in your possession; they will be released out in the world to visit geocaches!

2.6 Other Gear

Besides the equipment essential to geocaching, you should carry additional gear on your trip. The choice of what to take with you depends on the type of caches you plan to visit.

What to Carry

You should get a good map of the local area. This item is essential if your GPSr is not able to display a map, but it's helpful to have a separate map, since using the map function on some GPS receivers can be a heavy drain on the battery. Most paper maps and some digital ones show approximate latitude and longitude marks, which is often very helpful to the geocacher. Use your map to navigate roadways and especially to find barriers ahead of time. Nothing is more frustrating for a geocacher than to be within a couple of hundred feet of a cache—across an impassable stream! If your local map is a bulky book of city streets, you may find it practical to leave it in the car once you park. If you have a small, easy-to-fold map, you can take it with you all the way to the cache.

A magnetic compass uses the earth's magnetic field to find the direction that is approximately north. Directions from your magnetic compass and your GPSr may be slightly different because your GPSr uses the direction of true north, not magnetic north. (Some GPS receivers, however, also include an electronic version of a magnetic compass.) In general, the further north your latitude, the less accurate a magnetic compass will be. Despite the slight discrepancy, a magnetic compass can be a valuable tool for a geocacher.

The next most important item is a pen. A small weather–resistant pen from an outdoors or sporting goods shop is ideal, but you don't necessarily need the Cadillac of pens. You just need something to sign the log if a cache does not have a working pen or pencil inside it.

A small tool can be invaluable for certain geo-caches, and may occasionally be necessary for pulling out log sheets. Different types of tools can work; try tweezers or a small crochet hook. A multi-tool or Swiss army knife offers the most options and can be useful in other ways as well.

Pack any geocoins or travel bugs you currently have, as well as trade items. Don't forget this man-ual, which is designed to be lightweight and to fit into your pocket so you can take it with you.

Besides these items, you might bring any of the following, as well as a bag to carry it all in:

- Bottled water
- Field guides for local flora or fauna
- First aid kit
- Flashlight (great for searching crevices)
- Food (energy bars, trail mix, beef jerky, etc.)
- Hunting knife (follow local laws)
- Insect repellent
- Medications (epinephrine pens, inhalers, etc.)
- Mobile phone
- Rain poncho
- Spare batteries for your GPSr
- Sunglasses
- Sunscreen
- Trash bags for CITO
- Umbrella
- Whistle

What to Leave Behind

If you carry a purse, it's easiest to leave it at home, carrying only your identification and perhaps some cash. You may be getting in and out of the car frequently, and leaving anything valuable in the car is an invitation to thieves. Locking the vehicle is no protection against broken windows, and thieves may watch to see whether you hide anything.

Leaving electronics (besides your mobile phone and GPSr) at home is recommended. Part of the fun of geocaching is tuning in to the local environment as you follow the trail; MP3 players and gaming devices detract from the experience. They can also present a safety issue as well, leaving you less alert to your surroundings.

Pay attention to the weight of all your gear. Carrying a heavy load can be tiring, especially if you are not used to it.

What to Wear

Unless you plan to visit only urban park-and-grab caches (in which case street clothes are fine), dress for a trip to the outdoors. Your attire will be determined by the circumstances of your trip, but here are some general guidelines:

- Wear long pants, even in hot weather, to protect your legs from vegetation and insects.
- A wide-brimmed hat can protect your face from the sun, and UV-blocking sunglasses may be a good idea. However, remember that if there is heavy vegetation, your hat might get in the way.
- Wear sturdy, closed-toed shoes or hiking boots.

- If you have long hair, it will tend to get caught in branches even if it's tied back. Try wrapping it in a bandana.
- If weather is cold, wear layers for warmth. Use synthetic material, not cotton, if you might encounter wet conditions. Also pack a spare pair of socks if there is a chance your feet will get wet.

3 · Seeking Geocaches

Each geocache has several ratings that are important for the seeker to know: size, search difficulty, and terrain difficulty. If you are new to geocaching, start by looking for traditional caches that are small or regular in size and that have low search difficulty and terrain difficulty ratings.

Size indicates the size of the cache container. A "large" cache is about the size of a five-gallon bucket. A "regular" cache is about the size of a shoebox; an example is the ammo can. A "small" cache is about the size of a wallet; an example is a decon container. A "micro" cache is about the size of a medicine bottle or smaller. While technically considered micros, very tiny caches like blinkies are sometimes called nano caches or pico caches.

Search difficulty offers an idea of how well-hidden the geocache is. The ratings go from 1 to 5 stars, with increments of 0.5 stars. The higher the search difficulty rating, the more time you should expect to spend searching for the cache once you arrive at ground zero.

Terrain difficulty offers an idea of how long it will take for you to travel to ground zero on foot, and how challenging the hike will be. Terrain difficulty takes into account both the distance of the hike and the difficulty of crossing the ground itself. It uses the same scale as search difficulty. A cache with a terrain difficulty of 1 is accessible (or nearly so) to wheelchairs, while one with terrain difficulty 5 may take hours to reach, perhaps involving a very long hike or some expert climbing. Caches hidden in the woods typically have a terrain difficulty of two to four stars.

Drive as close as possible to the geocache or trailhead. Always park in a safe, legal location, even if it means walking farther. Your next step depends on the type of geocache you are pursuing.

3.1 Traditional Caches

Traditional caches are straightforward caches for which you are given the correct coordinates.

Micro cache hanging from a tree branch

There are no extra steps to take or waypoints to visit, and except for occasional tricky containers and difficult hides, no puzzles need to be solved. Some types of caches are especially common and present special challenges.

Park and Grab Caches (PNGs)

A "park and grab" is a geocache located in or near a parking area in an urban location. Usually

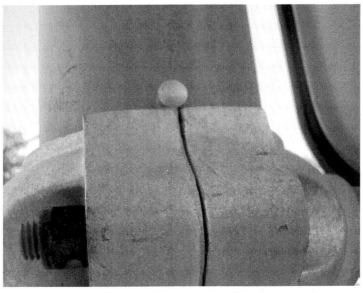

Round magnetic nano cache on a traffic signal post

stealth is necessary to avoid alarming the public. The most common site for PNGs is under the cover at the base of a light pole (a "skirt-lifter"). These covers are easily lifted up and conceal micro-sized cache containers. They also provide the container with a small amount of protection from the elements. Another possible location is a hole in a concrete parking curb (with the container typically attached to a piece of rebar or other metal). If there is a metal pole or fence nearby, check for magnetic caches. Sometimes geocaches are hidden, wrapped in camouflage duct tape, in the branches of a bush or tree in the landscaping.

Buildings

Caches located near buildings must be approached with caution because of the chance of getting unwanted attention. Tall buildings can both block and reflect satellite signals and cause strange GPSr readings. (GLONASS capability is a help in this regard because more satellite signals are available.) Remember that geocaches are always outdoors, never inside buildings!

City Parks

Geocaches are surprisingly common in public parks, despite the high traffic of pedestrians. Use stealth to avoid giving away the cache or alarming the public.

Trails

Undeveloped and wilderness areas are popular spots for geocaches. Usually they are placed in areas with marked trails, no more than a few feet from the trail itself. Follow the trail as close to the ground zero as possible. In the woods, trails can twist in unexpected directions, and often there is a better point just ahead along the trail from which you can start searching. Never go off the trail, no matter how tempting the geocache, if you must go more than a few feet or damage the surrounding environment. This practice is especially important in protected areas or in any area with signs that remind visitors to stay on the trail.

Follow good hiking safety practices. Be prepared for the possibility of bad weather, wildlife encounters, insect bites, and accidental falls. Always plan ahead for long hikes; these geocaches are not well suited to impulsive geocaching.

Finding geocaches in remote locations poses several challenges. First is the difficulty of the terrain. There may be steep drops or short climbs, and vegetation might get in the way. Approaching a cache through thick vegetation is called bushwhacking, which can present a real challenge in the form of thick brush and thorns.

Second, tree canopy can wreak havoc on the GPS signal strength. Ground zero may seem to jump all over the place. If this happens to you, try to find a clear spot to regain your bearings, and do your best to estimate the location of ground zero before you start your search in earnest.

Stream Beds

No matter what your GPSr says, a geocache is almost certainly not located in the dry bed of a stream or gully. Even if someone were foolish enough to hide one there, the cache would not last long because the current would sweep it away in the rain. Instead, look on the ground and in the vegetation along the banks. Exceptions may happen from time to time, with a very durable container tethered in the flow of a stream, and these situations should be explained in the online cache notes.

Bridges

If ground zero is near a bridge, the most likely hiding place is under the bridge. Searching out the cache is usually simple in the case of a foot bridge, but more complex in the case of something like a railroad trestle or highway overpass. Always use common sense and don't pursue caches that you cannot approach safely.

Cemeteries

Cemetery caches are popular because they provide a connection to the past. Sometimes a cache is hidden in honor of a loved one laid to rest

---

at that location. Park where appropriate and be respectful of the graves and of any mourners who might be present. Never disturb the graves even if it seems like that is where the cache is located.

3.2 Non-Traditional Caches

A non-traditional cache is a cache that has some sort of twist. There are several types of geocaches in this category.

Puzzle Caches

Also known as mystery caches, puzzle caches require you to solve some sort of puzzle in order to obtain the coordinates. Puzzle types range from sudoku to trivia questions to scavenger hunts. Finding a puzzle cache is a double achievement and some geocachers seek them out for this reason. The coordinates given for a puzzle cache are always near the actual coordinates, but are not the real coordinates. Never try to seek a puzzle cache from the given coordinates!

Multi-Caches

A multi-cache is a series of two or more caches or waypoints (coordinates without caches). In order to find the final cache and complete the series, a geocacher must find the preceding waypoints in the series. Several variations of multi-caches are commonly found. Sometimes each member of the series is itself a geocache and contains the coordinates for the next cache in the series; sometimes each stage except the final (which is always a regular geocache) is a tag, sticker, or magnet that includes the coordinates for the next stage. Multi-caches may be serial (in which each stage contains the coordinates for the next stage) or parallel (in which each stage contains part of the final coordinates). One variety of multi-cache is called an offset cache. In an offset cache, each stage before the final requires you to figure out the coordinates based on hints found in the surrounding environment. For example, a phone number on a nearby sign may need to be converted into coordinates.

Other Non-Traditional Caches

Some non-traditional caches, like Earth Caches, work like traditional caches, but with a tie-in to raise awareness of something (such as earth science). An Event Cache is not really a geocache, but a gathering of geocachers at a given place and time, sometimes for a purpose such as CITO.

A few non-traditional geocache types have been retired from Geocaching.com, but old caches of these types have been "grandfathered" and allowed to remain on the site. Among these are Virtual Caches, which encourage you to visit a set of coordinates but have no physical container to find, and Webcam caches, in which the goal is to go to a location and be photographed by a webcam.

3.3 Geocaching Safety

Geocaching is generally a safe activity, but some common sense precautions will lessen the small amount of risk.

- Drive to the cache safely. Don't try to read your GPSr while driving. Pull over in a safe place to consult your GPSr, or bring a buddy to help navigate. Never stop in the middle of traffic, and park safely and legally when you arrive.

- Keep an eye on the weather so you are not caught on the trail when a storm arrives. Never go outside during an electrical storm; stay inside your car or in a building.

- Watch your step at all times to avoid stepping in a hole or falling from a height.

- Stay away from anywhere there is a risk of falling into a body of water. Even if you are able to swim, you may have trouble with currents and be weighed down by clothes and shoes.

- Take care of your body. Stay hydrated, using sports drinks in hot weather to replenish lost electrolytes. Know your limits regarding long hikes.

- Be aware of others, especially vehicles, bicyclists, etc. In urban areas, watch out for stray dogs.

- Carry a first aid kit, either in the car for park-and-grabs or on the trail for longer hikes.

- If you will be going far from home, bring a buddy or make sure someone knows where you are going. Take a mobile phone in case you get lost. If you get truly and hopelessly lost, you can use your GPSr to tell a friend or rescuer your exact location! But remember that mobile phones do not always work in very remote areas.

- In urban areas, trust your instincts and stay in parts of the city where you feel comfortable. Watch out for hazardous conditions near vacant buildings and abandoned lots, always staying aware of your physical surroundings.

- Follow good trail safety practices. Stay on the trail. Wear appropriate clothing for protection. Tuck pants legs into your socks and use insect repellent. Learn how to identify irritating plants like poison ivy. Be aware of whether the area you are entering has dangerous wildlife, including venomous snakes, and know how to handle a wildlife encounter.

- At ground zero, keep your wits about you. Don't stick your hand blindly into holes, and don't mess around with dangerous items like electrical boxes. Once you find a cache, don't get too distracted by the excitement of opening it up and signing the log.

3.4 Geocaching with Kids

Kids love geocaching, especially if they can find trade items to keep. A few things are important to remember when geocaching with kids.

- The best caches for kids are medium to large caches with trade items. The cache should have easy to medium terrain difficulty; the younger the child, the easier the trail must be. Micro caches without trade items are fine, but be prepared for some kids to lose patience with these meager finds! For adults, just finding the cache and signing the log is its own reward, but kids are typically interested in swag.

- Plan your trip ahead of time, searching online for appropriate caches and planning a route. Impulsive geocaching is less likely to end in a fun experience for kids with a low frustration tolerance.

- Be willing to turn back if the trail to the cache proves too difficult or dangerous for a child. There is always another, easier cache to try.

- When you arrive at the cache, make sure your entire group follows good etiquette. Children should learn that taking an item always requires leaving an item of similar value—whether that item is their own toy or an trinket supplied by an adult is up to you. Show them how to hide the cache exactly as you found it and to be courteous by picking up nearby trash, if necessary (CITO).

4 · Hiding Your Own Geocache

Many geocachers are not content merely to seek caches. After they have found a number of caches, they begin to dream of hiding their own.

No matter how eager you are to hide a cache, wait until you have experience finding at least 50 or more. This experience is valuable in knowing the best (and worst) practices for hiding your own cache.

4.1 What You Need

To hide your own geocache, you need a sturdy container and a logbook. You may also choose to protect your logbook with a plastic bag. Inside the cache you may place trade items and perhaps a pen or pencil for signing the log, if there is room.

You may need some way to camouflage the container.

Good Containers

A good caching container should be weather-resistant and absolutely waterproof. It should be simple to open (unless it is a field puzzle) and have a large enough opening to make it easy for visitors to retrieve the log. Never rely on a plastic zip-top bag to keep the log dry. Plastic bags tear easily and don't last long, and they won't protect any trade items anyway. Instead, make certain that your container is truly watertight.

Some geocache containers are ready to use off the shelf, but many need to be camouflaged first. Disguising the container can mean simply wrapping it in camo–printed duct tape, or constructing an elaborate disguise. For especially devious camouflage, a fake rock, fake pine cone, etc. cannot be beaten. Use a second durable container inside, rather than a flimsy plastic bag. Common containers, in roughly descending order of size, include the following:

- Ammunition box (ammo can): These rectangular metal boxes, available at military surplus stores, are designed to for carrying and storing

Ammo can

ammunition safely. They are water tight because each one has a rubber gasket and a
lever mechanism to compress it. The roomy
interiors are great for trade items.

- Decontamination container (decon kit): In the
military, these waterproof plastic cases hold
supplies for personal decontamination of chemical weapons. Minus the original contents, they
are great cache containers that can hold small
trade items.

- Beach case: These waterproof plastic containers are designed to keep personal effects dry
during water sports.

Bison tube geocache, with the letters
"FTF" (First to Find) visible on the log

- Magnetic key holder: Originally intended to hide spare keys, these magnetic boxes make passable geocache containers, though they are not always adequately watertight by themselves.

- Soda tube (test tube): These items are the "blanks" used to produce soda bottles, and look like large plastic test tubes with a soda-bottle cap.

- Prescription bottle: These brown plastic containers are used by pharmacies to hold distribute prescription medications to customers. They are water-resistant but not absolutely waterproof and are best used for PNGs in protected sites.

- Matchstick container: Used by campers, these waterproof plastic capsules also make good micro caches.
- Film canister: These plastic canisters, smaller than prescription pill bottles, were originally used to hold 35mm film. They are uncommon now that digital cameras are popular, but can be found occasionally. They are best used for PNGs in protected locations.
- Metal capsule (Bison tube): Originally intended to let people carry medications on their key rings, these little metal tubes are made waterproof by an O-ring and make great micro caches. The name "Bison tube" is taken from the name of one manufacturer, Bison Designs of Longmont, Colorado. Not all metal capsules are tube-shaped; some are spherical, and others are hex-sided.
- Micro vial: Used in chemistry and biology labs, these little plastic vials look like inch-long clear plastic cones. They can be attached any sort of larger object to hide a geocache log.

- Magnetic button (blinky): Designed to accommodate a light-emitting diode (LED), these also can hold tiny geocaching logs.

A puzzle container or puzzle box is a device, often homemade, that requires a trick to open. These caches may be called "field puzzles." For example, a cache might be constructed of PVC pipe and require the opening of a valve to cause the container to fall out. Use your imagination and ingenuity to devise a puzzle box for a geocache, but avoid materials like wood that are vulnerable to the elements.

Bad Containers

Any container not absolutely waterproof, or unable to stand up to sun and rain for a long time, is a poor choice. Also avoid any container that encourages vandalism. Here are some examples of containers to avoid:

- Disposable food-storage containers (not waterproof)
- Naked plastic bag (not durable)
- Containers made from fragile materials like glass
- Fake sprinkler heads, electrical boxes, etc. Geocachers should never be encouraged to potentially vandalize property, nor to look in places

that may be dangerous. If these types of caches were common, geocachers would look for them more often, causing damage or getting electrocuted in the process.

- Fake dog poop. Encouraging geocachers to examine feces is poor etiquette.

Where to Get a Container

Various types of containers may be found from any of these sources:

- Military surplus store
- Online retailer or auction site
- Discount department store such as Wal-Mart
- Outdoors store
- Scouting store

Camouflage

The type of camouflage needed for the container depends on where it will be hidden. Containers that are well-hidden in enclosed sites (like under a lamp post cover) may not need any additional camouflage at all. The two most common means of camouflage are paint and duct tape. Many colors and designer prints of duct tape are available on the market today. Black tape will disguise any container stashed in a dark place.

Containers placed in fields or woods are often covered with camouflage-patterned duct tape, of the styles favored by the military or by hunters. Duct tape can also be matched by color to the background where it will be placed; for example, tan for a wood fence or silver for a chain-link fence. Another options is to glue rocks, mulch chips, or other materials to the outside of the container, or to fashion a cover (such as a hollow log) for the container. Be creative in disguising your geocache.

Logbooks

For large caches, use a notepad or small notebook for a log so visitors have plenty of room to sign. For micro caches, it's important that the log not be too large so that visitors can replace it easily. Micro logs therefore fill up faster and must be replaced more often than large cache logs.

Eventually, every container is likely to get some water in it. Geocachers may not always seal even the best container tightly, and sometimes the waterproof seals deteriorate. Therefore, the log-book needs to be protected from water. Many geocachers rely on plastic bags, but these have a very short lifespan and often are not resealed properly by visitors. The best strategy is to use waterproof paper from a company like Rite in the Rain. Water-proof notebooks, some designed explicitly for geo-caching, can be purchased from outdoors stores or from the Internet.

Along with the log, it's a good idea to leave a note identifying your container as a geocache. A sample note, which you may copy and use in your caches, is found on page 75.

4.2 How to Place Your Cache

Don't place caches randomly just for the sake of having a large number of geocaches to your name; each one should have some purpose, whether to share some important part of local history or just to enrich an area that doesn't have many caches. Your cache must be placed at least 1/10 mile (528 feet) from the nearest existing cache.

Good Locations

There is no end to the number of good hiding places for a geocache. Here are a few examples of great hiding places for caches:

- Within a hollow at the base of a tree
- In a crevice between rocks
- Under the cover at the base of a lamp post

Bad place for a geocache

- Hanging from the branches of a small tree or bush
- On a metal surface to which a magnetic cache can be attached
- Inside a piece of semi-permanent debris such as a concrete pipe
- Under the cap of a fence post (if it can be removed easily without damaging the fence)

Bad Locations

Not every location is appropriate for a geocache. Use common sense, and always avoid all of the following:

- Any place posted "no trespassing" or not legally accessible. Geocaches should only be placed in legal locations, which may require asking the property owner's permission. Not all caches you seek will follow these rules, but it's best if you do.
- Any area not accessible to the general public (for example, gated communities)
- Any spot where water or erosion may carry it away
- Open areas of abandoned fields or vacant lots (maintenance crews may sweep it away)
- Landscaped areas (maintenance crews will throw it out if they find it)
- Dangerous or high-crime areas
- Any place that requires disturbing a grave. Cemetery caches are great, but geocaches should not be placed under grave stones, in flower vases, etc.

5 · Useful Information

5.1 How to Find a Geocache

Get as close to ground zero as possible. On cloudy days or under heavy tree cover, the GPS receiver may have trouble getting a signal, and as a result, ground zero will seem to jump around. In that case, make your best guess as to the general location of ground zero.

Once you have a good idea of where ground zero is, start looking for nearby hiding places. Don't just look for the cache itself; it's hidden and camouflaged! Make use of any information you have, such as a hint or log entries made by other geocachers, and keep in mind the size and probable type of the container you are seeking.

Look in crevices, in tree branches, under covering items, and anywhere else that might hide a cache.

Range outward in a spiral from ground zero up to a radius of 30 feet or more, to allow for imprecision in the GPS coordinates. The coordinates will be less accurate if there is anything (buildings, trees, clouds) to interfere with the satellite signals.

Finding Ground Zero Without Entering Coordinates

You may have a GPS receiver that won't let you manually enter coordinates. If it will tell you your current latitude and longitude, you can still use it to find puzzle caches, multi-caches, and any other cache whose coordinates you cannot upload to your device. A magnetic compass separate from your GPSr is very useful.

Find the approximate location of the cache on a map and go to that location.

Turn on your GPSr and see how far you are (in degrees) from each of the coordinates.

Use your compass to travel north or south, and east or west, toward the coordinates. This step is the one in which having a separate magnetic compass is helpful. If you don't have a separate compass, toggle if necessary between your GPSr's compass and position information.

Use this method to home in on the cache coordinates. This is ground zero.

Finding a Cache Without a GPSr

Considering the nature of geocaching, it would seem impossible to find a cache without a GPS receiver. But a few simple caches can be found by an experienced geocacher using only a map. If you would like to try this activity, select a very easy park-and-grab cache. Go to the approximate location and look for likely hiding places. For example, if the coordinates seem to be near a parking lot, check for light-pole caches in the lot.

5.2 Conversions

Geocachers sometimes find it useful to convert the abstract units of degrees to another, more practical format. You might, for instance, have a coordinate in decimal degrees and a GPSr that only accepts a degrees and minutes format. You might even want to know just how large a distance is represented by a degree.

How to Convert Coordinate Formats

Latitude and longitude may be given in either of two formats: decimal degrees or in degrees and minutes. A coordinate in decimal degrees takes the form of a single number, either positive or negative, with about five decimal places. A coordinate in degrees and minutes consists of a positive whole number, a degree sign (°), a number with about three decimal places, a single apostrophe ('), and a letter indicating direction (N, S, E, W).

To convert from decimal degrees to degrees and minutes, take only the decimal portion of the number, including the decimal point, and multiply it by 60. Use this number as the minutes portion, following the whole number of degrees. A positive decimal degree coordinate becomes north for latitude or east for longitude; a negative coordinate becomes south for latitude or west for longitude. For example, to convert the longitude -95.56344 to degrees and minutes, multiply 0.56344 by 60 to get 33.806. Since the original coordinate is negative, it's in the western hemisphere. The coordinate in degrees and minutes, then, is 95° 33.806' W.

To convert from degrees and minutes to decimal degrees, take just the minutes portion and divide it by 60. The result will always be a number between 0 and 1. Add this result to the degrees to get the decimal degrees. Make it a negative number if it's in the southern or western hemisphere. For example, to convert the latitude the latitude 29° 47.877' N to decimal degrees, divide 47.877 by 60 to get 0.79793. Since the original coordinate is north, the decimal degree is a postive number. The coordinate in decimal degrees, then, is 29.79793°.

How to Convert Latitude and Longitude to Distance

Latitude and longitude represent imaginary lines on the round earth, not exact distances. However, approximate conversions can be made. For latitude, these conversions are approximately the same at any latitude and longitude. For longitude, because all the meridians are great circles that pass through the poles, the conversions are different at every latitude. The approximate conversions for several latitudes are given in the tables on the next pages. Round off your estimate based on your latitude.

Latitude:

1 minute = 1842.9m = 6046 feet or 1.15 mile

0.01 minute = about 60 feet

1 degree = about 68.7 miles

0.01 degree = 3627 feet

0.0001 degree = about 36 feet

Longitude at the equator:

1 minute = 1855.2m = 6086 feet or 1.15 mile

0.01 minute = about 61 feet

1 degree = about 69.2 miles

0.01 degree = 3652 feet

0.0001 degree = about 37 feet

Longitude at 30° latitude:

1 minute = 1605.6m = 5267 feet or 1.00 mile

0.01 minute = about 53 feet

1 degree = about 59.9 miles

0.01 degree = 3160 feet

0.0001 degree = about 32 feet

Longitude at 51° 28' (Greenwich, England):

1 minute = 1153.2m = 3783 feet or 0.72 mile

0.01 minute = about 38 feet

1 degree = about 43.0 miles

0.01 degree = 2270 feet

0.0001 degree = about 23 feet

Longitude at 60° latitude:

1 minute = 925.2m = 3035 feet or 0.57 mile

0.01 minute = about 30 feet

1 degree = about 34.5 miles

0.01 degree = 1821 feet

0.0001degree = about 18 feet

ROT13 Key

On Geocaching.com, potential spoilers are en-coded using a cipher called ROT13. Each letter stands for the letter exactly 13 places before or af-ter it in the alphabet. Use this key to decipher ROT13.

```
a  b  c  d  e  f  g  h  i  j  k  l  m
N  O  P  Q  R  S  T  U  V  W  X  Y  Z


n  o  p  q  r  s  t  u  v  w  x  y  z
A  B  C  D  E  F  G  H  I  J  K  L  M
```

5.3 Miscellaneous

How to Explain Yourself to Outsiders

Eventually, you are likely to be questioned by someone (perhaps a passerby, or perhaps a police officer or security guard) as to what you are doing. Explaining geocaching to the uninitiated is notorious for producing confusion and suspicion. If this happens to you, be ready to explain that you are on a scavenger hunt using GPS. This easy response tells your questioner that your intentions are innocent and explains why you may be acting in a way that seems unusual.

How to Make a Geocaching Bag From a Bandana

You can make a handy, easy-to-carry bag from a cotton bandana, a truly economical choice. Bandanas are available at hobby stores and discount stores for as little as $1.00. Unlike a drawstring bag or a backpack, this bag lies open when the top flaps are untied so all the contents are easy to see.

1. Lay the bandana out right side up on a flat surface.
2. Turn one corner diagonlly to the far corner to form a triangle.

Bandana Bag

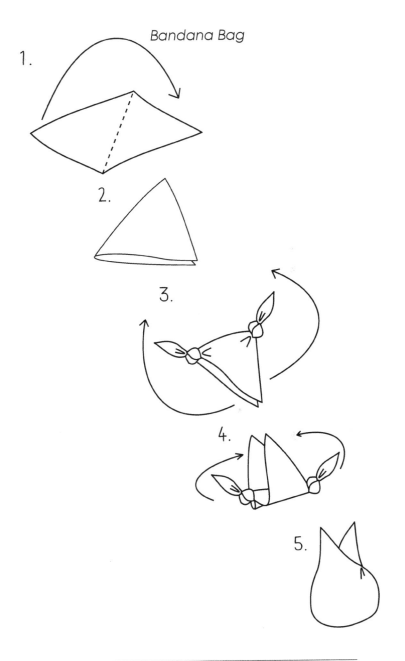

3. About one third of the way from the end of one short side of the triangle, tie an overhand knot. Repeat for the other short side. Turn the bag right side out.
4. Tuck the the knots inside.
5. Fill the bag with your pen, trade items, etc. Use a square knot (two half knots) to tie the two free corners of the bag closed.

Note to Place in Your Geocaches

Occasionally "muggles" who are unaware of geoaching will find a cache. You may copy the note on the following page to place in your cache. It explains the game of geocaching and invites whoever finds the note to join in the hobby of geocaching.

THIS IS A GEOCACHE

This container and its contents are a geocache, part of an international <u>scavenger hunt game</u> that uses GPS technology. Geocaching is a treasure-seeking game where the map is based on the Global Positioning System. If you found this container by accident, you're invited to join in! Here's how:

<u>Sign your name</u> or handle on the enclosed log, along with the date. Then create an account at http://www.geocaching.com, where you can record your find online.

Please replace this container <u>exactly where you found it</u>. Please do not modify or vandalize it in any way.

Feel free to take any items you find in this container, but only if you <u>leave something of equal (or greater) value behind</u>. These items are for trade and for fun!

We're glad you found this cache!

Thanks for playing!

Glossary

ammo can: A waterproof metal ammunition box used by the military to store and transport ammunition.

beach case: A waterproof plastic case the size of a wallet, used to protect wallet contents during water sports.

Bison tube: A metal capsule, about one to three inches in length, that may be used as geocache container.

blinky: A magnetic light the size of a large pill, made to accommodate a button battery and single light-emitting diode (LED). With the electronics removed, these are sometimes used as nano caches.

BYOP: "Bring your own pen."

Cache In Trash Out: 1. The habit of cleaning up the area when visiting caches. 2. A community event for cleaning up the areas around geo-caches.

CITO: "Cache In Trash Out."

coordinate: Either of the two numbers used to indicate a location on the earth's surface. A coordinate measures either latitude or longitude, and two coordinates are needed to specify a location.

decimal degrees: A convention used for specifying coordinates. In decimal degrees, a positive number indicate a latitude north of the equator or a longitude east of the prime meridian. A negative number indicates a latitude south of the equator or a longitude west of the prime meridian.

decon container: A military-issued waterproof plastic container about the size of a hand, designed to carry supplies for neutralizing chemical weapons. The containers are often used for geo-caches.

degree: 1/360 of the diameter of a circle or sphere.

degrees and minutes: A convention used for specifying coordinates. Whether a latitude is north or south of the equator, or a longitude east or west of the prime meridian, is indicated following the numerical coordinate by the letter N, S, E, or W, respectively.

DNF: "Did not find."

equator: An imaginary great circle on the earth that is exactly the same distance from the north and south poles. Locations north of the equator are in the northern hemisphere, and locations south of it are in the southern hemisphere.

FTF: "First to find."

geocoin: A metal coin-like trackable item printed with a serial number and able to be tracked on a site like Geocaching.com.

geographic north pole: The point at the north end of the earth's axis. This is the direction indicated as north by the Global Positioning System, but not by magnetic compasses, which track magnetic north.

GPS: "Global Positioning System."

GPSr: "Global Positioning System receiver." The device used to acquire and display one's location according to the satellite-based Global Positioning System.

great circle: a circle drawn around a sphere (such as the globe) that has the same diameter of the sphere; the largest possible circle that can be drawn on a sphere.

ground zero: The location specified by a geo-cache's coordinates. At ground zero, the GPSr will typically indicate that the geocacher is "0 feet" or "0 meters" from the cache.

Groundspeak: Owner of geocaching.com, the most prominent geocaching website.

GZ: "Ground zero."

latitude: The distance, measured in degrees, of a location from the equator. Latitude measurements must indicate whether they are north or south of the equator. The distance from the equator to the location is measured along an imaginary great circle, so the distance measured by each degree of latitude is approximately constant regardless of location.

log: A record of visits to a geocache. "Log" can refer either to the paper log (a notebook or sheet of paper found in a geocache, used by each visitor to record their name and the date of the visit), or to the electronic log, maintained on the geocache's web page and updated by each user who finds the cache.

longitude: The distance, measured in degrees, of a location from the prime meridian. The distance from the prime meridian to the location is measured along an imaginary circle parallel to the equator, so each the distance measured by each degree of longitude varies depending on latitude.

magnetic north: The direction toward the magnetic north pole. Depending on your location, magnetic north is usually close to, but not exactly the same as, true north.

magnetic north pole: The point at which the earth's magnetic field points downward toward the earth. At the time of publishing, the location of the magnetic north pole is about N 82° 18' N, 113° 24' W, in the Arctic Sea about 570 miles south of the true north pole, and is moving westward at a rate of 34 to 37 miles per year.

micro cache: A geocache smaller than a person's hand, generally too small to accommodate anything but a log and perhaps a few miniature trade items.

minute: A unit of latitude or longitude equal to 1/60 of a degree.

multi-cache: A series of caches or waypoints, in which finding previous entries in the series is necessary in order to find the final cache.

nano cache: An exceptionally small micro cache, large enough only for a tiny piece of log paper. A blinky is a type of nano cache.

offset cache: A multi-cache in which the stages before the final rely on hints found in the surrounding environment.

paperless geocaching: The practice of using geocache description and log information stored in a GPS receiver or other electronic device instead of printed on paper.

park and grab: A geocache, usually urban, located in or very close to a parking area.

Pathtag: A signature trade item commissioned by some geocachers. Though serially numbered like trackables, and able to be registered online, Pathtags may be collected like other trade items.

pico cache: An exceedingly small micro cache, generally thought of as being the size of or smaller than a nano.

PNG: "Park and grab."

Pocket Query: A file generated from Geocaching.com containing data on up to 1000 caches.

prime meridian: An imaginary line on the earth's surface stretching from the north pole to the south pole and passing through Greenwich, England. Locations within 180 degrees east of the prime meridian are in the eastern hemisphere, and those within 180 degrees west of it are in the western hemisphere.

puzzle cache: A geocache that requires the solution of some sort of puzzle in order to obtain the complete coordinates.

signal strength: A measure of the number of satellites a GPSr is currently tracking, and of the strength of those signals.

skirt-lifter: A park-and-grab located under the loose cover at the base of a light pole.

swag: Trade items.

TFTC: "Thanks for the cache"

TFTH: "Thanks for the hide"

trackable: A object (either a geocoin or a Travel Bug) moved by various players from cache to cache, with the movements recorded online.

Travel Bug: A type of trackable item that is a trademark of Groundspeak.

true north: The direction toward the geographic north pole.

waypoint: A location, indicated by coordinates, that may be used as a help in navigating somewhere, such as to a geocache.

Index

Field Notes

Credits

Except where otherwise noted, all text, photographs, and illustrations are the work of the author.

Neither the author nor the publisher are affiliated with Geocaching.com nor with any other geocaching website.

The illustration of the Block IIR(M) GPS satellite found on page 5 is a work of the U.S. government available at http://www.gps.gov and is in the public domain.

The Geocachers' Creed was developed by the greater geocaching community and can be found at www.geocreed.info. Reprinted under the terms of the Creative Commons Attribution-No Derivatives Generic License 2.0 (http://creativecommons.org/licenses/by-nd/2.0/).

Magnetic north pole coordinates were taken from http://www.findlatitudeandlongitude.com/

The sources for information specific to Geocaching.com are Groundspeak's websites http://www.geocaching.com, http://forums.groundspeak.com/GC/, and http://support.groundspeak.com.

Made in the USA
Lexington, KY
16 May 2013